Superstars
of the
DALLAS
COWBOYS

by Matt Scheff

amicus
high interest

Amicus High Interest is published by Amicus
P.O. Box 1329, Mankato, MN 56002
www.amicuspublishing.us

Library of Congress Cataloging-in-Publication Data
Scheff, Matt.
  Superstars of the Dallas Cowboys / Matt Scheff.
      pages cm. -- (Pro sports superstars)
  Includes index.
  ISBN 978-1-60753-523-2 (hardcover) -- ISBN 978-1-60753-553-9 (eBook)
  1. Dallas Cowboys (Football team)--History--Juvenile literature.
  2. Football players--United States--Biography--Juvenile literature. I. Title.
  GV956.D3S3 2014
  796.332'64092812--dc23
                        2013006857

Photo Credits: Evan Pinkus/AP Images, cover; Marc Serota/AP Images, 2,
17; David Drapkin/AP Images, 5; NFL Photos/AP Images, 6, 9, 13; Nick Ut/
AP Images, 10; Greg Trott/AP Images, 14; Rusty Kennedy/AP Images, 18,
22; Scott Boehm/AP Images, 21

Produced for Amicus by The Peterson Publishing Company
and Red Line Editorial.

Editor Jenna Gleisner
Designer Becky Daum
Printed in the United States of America
Mankato, MN
July, 2013
PA 1938
10 9 8 7 6 5 4 3 2 1

TABLE OF CONTENTS

Meet the Dallas Cowboys   4

Bob Lilly   6

Roger Staubach   8

Tony Dorsett   10

Randy White   12

Michael Irvin   14

Troy Aikman   16

Emmitt Smith   18

DeMarcus Ware   20

Team Fast Facts   22

Words to Know   23

Learn More   24

Index   24

MEET THE DALLAS COWBOYS

The Dallas Cowboys joined the **NFL** in 1960. They have gone to eight Super Bowls. They won five of them. Dallas has had many great players. Here are some of the best.

BOB LILLY

Bob Lilly was great at **defense**. It took two men to block him. Lilly went to 11 **Pro Bowls**. He helped the Cowboys win a Super Bowl.

Lilly was the Cowboys' first draft pick in 1961.

ROGER STAUBACH

Roger Staubach was a great **quarterback**. He had a strong arm. He went to four Super Bowls. The Cowboys won two of them in 1972 and 1978. Many fans think he is the best Cowboy ever.

TONY DORSETT

Tony Dorsett was a smooth runner. He could dart past tacklers. He was tough to catch. He was the **Rookie** of the Year in 1977. He was the Cowboys' top runner ten years in a row!

Dorsett once ran 99 yards. That is the longest run of all time in the NFL.

RANDY WHITE

Randy White was a great defender. He played hard. White missed only one game in 14 seasons. He went to three Super Bowls. He was a Super Bowl **MVP** in 1978.

MICHAEL IRVIN

Michael Irvin was hard to stop. He was big and fast. He was great at catching the ball. He helped the Cowboys win three Super Bowls. He played in five Pro Bowls.

Irvin was the Pro Bowl MVP in 1992.

TROY AIKMAN

Troy Aikman was a great quarterback. He could throw quick and short passes. Or he could throw long ones. He helped Dallas win three Super Bowls. Aikman went to six Pro Bowls in a row starting in 1991.

EMMITT SMITH

Emmitt Smith was not the biggest or fastest runner. But he was smart. He knew how to use his blockers. Smith helped the Cowboys win three Super Bowls.

Smith broke the record for career rushing yards in 2002.

DEMARCUS WARE

DeMarcus Ware can crash through blockers. Or he can run around them. Ware had the most **sacks** in 2008 and 2010. He may one day beat the NFL record.

The Cowboys have had many great stars. Who will be the next?

TEAM FAST FACTS

Founded: 1960

Nicknames: America's Team, The Boys

Home Stadium: Cowboys Stadium (Arlington, Texas)

Super Bowl Titles: 5 (1971, 1977, 1992, 1993, and 1995)

Hall of Fame Players: 14, including Bob Lilly, Roger Staubach, Tony Dorsett, Randy White, Michael Irvin, Troy Aikman, and Emmitt Smith

WORDS TO KNOW

defense – the group of players that tries to stop the other team from scoring

MVP – Most Valuable Player; an honor given to the best player each season

NFL – National Football League; the league pro football players play in

Pro Bowl – the NFL's all-star game

quarterback – a player whose main jobs are to lead the offense and throw passes

rookie – a player in his first season

sack – a tackle of the quarterback on a passing play

LEARN MORE

Books

Caffrey, Scott. *The Story of the Dallas Cowboys*. Mankato, MN: Creative Paperbacks, 2010.

Heits, Rudolph T. *DeMarcus Ware*. Philadelphia: Mason Crest Publishers, 2011.

Web Sites

Dallas Cowboys—Official Site
http://www.dallascowboys.com
Watch video clips and view photos of the Dallas Cowboys.

NFL.com
http://nfl.com
Check out pictures and your favorite football players' stats.

NFL Rush
http://www.nflrush.com
Play games and learn how to be a part of NFL PLAY 60.

INDEX

Aikman, Troy, 16

Dorsett, Tony, 11

Irvin, Michael, 15

Lilly, Bob, 7

MVP, 15

NFL, 4, 11, 20

Pro Bowls, 7, 15, 16

Smith, Emmitt, 19
Staubach, Roger, 8
Super Bowls, 4, 7, 8, 12, 15, 16, 19

Ware, DeMarcus, 20
White, Randy, 12